Howl for the Vanished

B.D. Lynn
Edited by Shana Rinderle

Dedication

For the red wolves—
whose howls are the last anthem of a fading wild,
marked by scars, hunted by shadow and silence.
Yet they endure, barely,
their cry our shared call
against forgetting, against vanishing.

Read. Remember.
Then rise up—
for the rarest canid, howling for kin—
though none ever hear.

Introduction

This isn't just poetry.
It's blood on the page.

I don't write for critics—
those who study pain they've never felt
from a safe distance.

I come from nights that never ended,
and losses no one could fix.
I come from where you come from.

I write for the ones still carrying it—

Men with heavy hands
and heavier hearts.
Women who hold grief
like heirlooms passed down.

Outlaws. Ghosts.
Quiet fighters too stubborn to fall.

I don't write to impress.
I write to reach.

If your scars tell stories,
this book was always yours.

—B.D. Lynn

The Ledger

1. I'm Always There .... Page 1
2. Wolves in the Wreckage .... Page 4
3. White Petals ....Page 6
4. Remembering Grace .... Page 7
5. I'll Walk On .... Page 9
6. Marked .... Page 11
7. No Alter Needed..................................... Page 12
8. Rules of the Mountain .... Page 15
9. The Ember .... Page 21
10. Beyond the Weathered Gate................. Page 23
11. Scars .... Page 25
12. Between You and the Dark .... Page 28
13. Red Wolf's Vow .... Page 30
14. I Don't Sleep .... Page 32
15. Aftermath .... Page 33
16. Devoured .... Page 36
17. Bitter Streams .... Page 38
18. Masks of Sin .... Page 40
19. The Frogs Sing Anyway .... Page 42
20. Unshaken .... Page 44
21. Red Wolf's Kin .... Page 46
22. The Hum .... Page 48
23. Held What Broke Better Men .... Page 51
24. Loyalty Is Quiet .... Page 53
25. Porchlight .... Page 55

26. You Saw a Lantern .... Page 58
27. Bittersweet Realization .... Page 60
28. Tides of Eternal Night .... Page 61
29. Smiling for the Strings .... Page 62
30. Standing on Ruins .... Page 64
31. The Void .... Page 66
32. Certainty's End .... Page 68
33. Heavens Haze .... Page 70
34. Where the Honeysuckle Grows .... Page 72
35. Red Wolf's Ghost .... Page 74
36. Old Souls .... Page 76
37. Middle of the End .... Page 78
38. I Stayed .... Page 80
39. Under These Oaks .... Page 83
40. Still Breathing .... Page 86
41. What a Man Ought To .... Page 88
42. Spark to Cinder .... Page 90
43. Bloodshot Dawns .... Page 92
44. Morgan Dollars .... Page 94
45. Clear Sky .... Page 96
46. Howl for the Vanished .... Page 99

Howl for the Vanished
I'm Always There

When the time comes
that I've spent the last of mine—
don't waste any of yours
pining over me.

Don't shed a tear,
before long I'll be near.
I'm not fit for Heaven's choir,
and Hell don't want my kind of fire.

No wings for me,
no chain, no crown,
I won't stay still, I won't stay down.
So don't weep, don't waste your breath,
I never feared a thing like death.

I'll be the creak of your floor,
the lock that holds your front door.
The stillness right before you speak.
The strength that finds you,
when you're weak.

Howl for the Vanished

Heaven called, but I said "not yet."
Some folks I love still walk this land,
and they still need my steady hand.

No wings. No harp. No shining gate.
I'm not in Heaven, I can wait.
Not because I'm damned-
I didn't fall from grace,
I simply love you too much not to stay.

You'll feel me when the nights get cold,
when shadows stretch and fear takes hold.
I'll be the step behind your own,
the reason you never feel alone.

I won't say much, I never did.
Kept love buried since I's a kid.
But real love don't need to shout,
it shows up when you're down and out.

Howl for the Vanished

If you break, or lose hope,
I'll be the feeling that helps you cope.
The whisper in your quiet fight,
"Keep going, kid. You'll be all right."

The shadow flickering in the hall,
The chill that makes your skin crawl,
a whisper through the midnight air,
All just me-reminding you,
I'm always there.

Howl for the Vanished
Wolves in the Wreckage

I wasn't looking when you found me,
standing in the haze of my own making—
you pierced the poison I breathed like penance,
cut through the steel I wore like armor,
down to the grotto
where I guard the boy
who lost his innocence
long before he lost his baby teeth.

Yet there you stood—
grinning like a kid
who just stole something
and got away clean.

No halo,
nowhere near saintly—
but marked by your own fire,
not to heal me,
only to see.

Howl for the Vanished

So don't call it love—
call it collision,
like two wolves catching scent
through the wreckage of superstition.

You weren't my savior—
just the first to stay,
when I bared all the ruin
and didn't look away.

Howl for the Vanished
White Petals

The fire in your blood didn't flicker—it raged,
lit your eyes like hell come early,
while poison moved quiet, slow as sin,
playing the long game 'til it caved you in.

Your head told your heart, "Not now, not yet,"
but mercy don't answer an addict's regrets.
You dreamed of kids, porch swings, and peace—
visions forever out of reach.

I smelled bleach in that room,
heard death pacing the halls.
The haints knew your name.
The silence knew mine.
We used to drink shine under bruised-up skies—
now even the moon won't meet my eyes.

You swallowed white petals like they meant freedom,
but they bloomed like lies, rotting you from inside—
each one a needle, pulling me through
the same door I opened for you.
That wasn't healing. That was execution.

Howl for the Vanished

"Don't detox here," they said—
but you never did listen.
You burned too hot
for a thing like confliction,
too wild for their pity.
You went out like a match in a gasoline-drenched city.

I hope you're raising hell somewhere beyond bone,
throwing stars like punches, never alone.
But me? I'm still here—
same boots, same porch,
with your name carved deep in the wood,
raw as the ache I carry.

You were born marked holy—
and hunted for it.

The fire in your blood gave the dark its light.
But the poison?
It waited.
It knew how to fight.

Now I drink enough for us both,
cuss the sky 'til it splits like a vein,
pining your face in this Appalachian haze.

Howl for the Vanished
Remembering Grace

Our minds are new to each other,
yet our hearts
already share a secret tongue.

Maybe in a life long past,
or eons before history
began to breathe,
our souls were kindred fragments,
two pieces of one vast,
unfolding design,
destined to find their way home.

Your whiskey brown eyes
are a familiar echo,
a whisper from a forgotten dream.
They tell me we've been here before,
together in some blissful, forgotten place.

Meeting you isn't a beginning,
It's remembering grace.

Howl for the Vanished
I'll Walk On

Every candle you light,
sputtering in the dark—
won't fill the void.

Every prayer you whisper—
words spilling like water
from shattered glass,
can't stitch the tear.

There's a hole now,
raw-edged,
where your laugh used to echo—
where your voice curled like smoke
from your last cigarette.

It's empty.

No flame,
no murmured hope,
can carve you back into being.

Just this—

Howl for the Vanished

a gut-shot lull in the early hours,
a silence that bites.
And me,
staring at the space
where you used to be.

But in the ache—
a relentless pulse.

Time turns,
and I'll walk on,
carrying the weight.

Howl for the Vanished
Marked

Most shuffle the earth with soft feet,
their days a slow fade in gray—
no ripples, no fires,
just dust and dirt
waiting to take them back.

They cling to comfort
like children to nightlights,
turn away from the bite of the wind,
their dreams dissolving,
trickling down quiet streets
into drains no one remembers.

But there are some—
some who walk like rivers cut through rock,
shoulders squared, hearts clear as glass.
They take the storm's tongue
and let it carve their name—
a mark, a testament
that they lived,
that they stood tall in the silence,
and made the earth remember them.

Howl for the Vanished
No Alter Needed

I never felt like I needed the holy men—
their voices too soft,
their hands too clean.
I've seen the world's teeth,
felt the cold bite of nights
that don't end,
even when you're begging them to.

I've got scars I don't bother counting,
knuckles split from fights
I couldn't walk away from,
and a silence in my chest
that's louder
than any prayer they could preach.

But still—
I feel Him in the marrow of me,
in the weight of my boots on hard ground,
in the blood that never stops
pounding through these tired veins.

Howl for the Vanished

I don't speak His name
like a beggar's plea—
I keep it in the back of my throat,
a rough-edged vow
that don't need words.
I see Him in the beauty of dawn
over cold earth,
in the sweat that stings my eyes
when the sun's high and unrelenting.

They say you need saving—
I reckon I've been saved a hundred times.
Each morning I rise
and breathe in the dirt and the dust,
each night I sit with the weight
of my own mistakes
and still find a spark
that won't go out.

I'm not one for churches—
the wood pews and the polished stone
don't speak to me like the wind does,
like the hush of dusk settling in
around a man who's fought
for every breath he's got left.

Howl for the Vanished

I don't kneel easy—
my knees are too worn
from holding the world's weight,
and there's only ever been one man
I'd kneel for—
and He don't need no pulpit
to see the truth in me.

Some men find God
in the quiet spaces
between each ragged breath,
in the dirt under their fingernails,
in the long nights
when they're too tired to fight
but too proud to surrender.

And that's enough—
to feel Him
in the calloused hands,
the cracked voice,
the battered heart
that still won't quit.
Some men don't need no altar—
just the promise
that in the hush between each breath,
they are not alone.

Howl for the Vanished

RULES OF THE MOUNTAIN
(Passed down in hush and holler)

Howl for the Vanished

If you hike where the fog clings low to the pine,
And the wind through the holler hums mournful in time,
Then heed what the old ones have carved into lore,
Or you won't leave the woods
like you've left them before.

Howl for the Vanished

WARNING I
When daylight is dying, be back in your bed,
For dusk stirs the ones who remember the dead.

WARNING II
Don't open for knocking, don't answer your name,
If it stands on two legs but don't move the same.

WARNING III
If you hear a soft song where no singer should be,
Keep walking and humming, eyes down—
don't you dare see.

Howl for the Vanished

WARNING IV
Leave bread on the stump if you've borrowed the trail,
Or the Little Folk may curse you with more than just ail.

WARNING V
Don't wave at the figure that waits in the field,
It knows you've now seen it— it won't stay concealed.

WARNING VI
Don't speak of the thing that you glimpsed in the trees,
What's named becomes real, and it'll find you with ease.

Howl for the Vanished

WARNING VII
If silence falls sudden, then hush every breath—
The quiet in woods is the herald of death.

WARNING VIII
Three pennies at crossroads, don't ask—just obey,
Or you'll owe a fare that you can't ever pay.

WARNING IX
Don't cut at the oak with the face in the bark,
Its roots run through bones buried deep in the dark.

Howl for the Vanished

WARNING X
If a man joins your fire and won't meet your gaze,
Offer food, ask no questions,
and part ways with praise.

WARNING XI
Don't fish past the hour when the moon's at its height,
What bites past that mark drags you down out of sight.

WARNING XII
Mark ash on your door come the coldest of nights,
To ward off the shadows that dance without light.

Howl for the Vanished

WARNING XIII
If you wake with dirt on the soles of your feet,
Say thanks and lie down— don't recall, don't repeat.
For the journey you took was not of your will,
And the whisper you followed keeps beckoning still.

And pray—
not the way that the preacher man said—
But in the tongue of your mamaw,
hushed, mournful and low.

For only words of old can sever the ties
That bind you to shadows
beneath mountain skies.

Howl for the Vanished
The Ember

There's a fire in my chest
that wants to burn clean
I bury it under jokes
and cigarette smoke,
I tell it,
not now,
people are watching.

there's a fire in my chest
that wants to burn pure
but I drown it in
Whiskey and noise
and let the T.V. talk
so I don't have to.

The fire whispers things like:
call your mother,
forgive her,
Reach out more.

I tell it,
pipe down,
we've got bills to pay,
and a schedule to keep,
and nobody gives
a damn about
embers.

Howl for the Vanished

but sometimes
in the dark,
with no one around,
I crack a window
and let the wind touch it.

just enough,
to feel warm again,
without setting
the whole house on fire.

and we sleep like that,
me and the ember,
close,
but quiet.

Howl for the Vanished
Beyond the Weathered Gate

I came upon the weathered gate,
decades leaned against its weight.
The hinges wept, bare branches sighed—
the kind of place things come die.

She was here late last year,
when dusk drew close and snow was near.
She left her coat upon the rail,
as if she'd only gone too pale.

I told the town I'd made my peace,
but grief, once stirred, will never cease.

And so I walk where no lights go,
her name still trembling in my throat—
a fraying thread, a final note.

It cracks the cold. It splits the air.
But never brings her anywhere.

Each tree now stands the way she stood.
Each path bends deeper into wood.

I see her eyes in bark and stone—
they never blink. I'm getting cold.

Howl for the Vanished

I've cursed the sky. I've begged the ground.
I've screamed until no voice came out.

But all I hear is wind through pine
and thoughts that rot but won't resign.
I swore I'd leave a thousand times.
I swore I'd stop unearthing signs.

But love like this don't fade or sleep.
It just gets buried...
bone deep.

No voice replied. No shadow stirred.
Just wind—
not a single word.

Yet still I sit beneath the pine,
and soon her hand might reach for mine
as I go still...
where she lost her fight.

Howl for the Vanished
Scars

You said life's weight broke your heart cold,
Its burden a stone in a grief untold.
Each night, fears whispered through your mind,
Binding you tight in a dread undefined.

You cried on the floor,
where splinters bit,
Forced a smile through pain
though your strength felt split.
Clutching a heart torn but fierce with fight,
You pushed through the dark
with a stubborn light.

You swore love would never break your guard,
Your heart locked tight, scarred and battle-hard.

Then he came—
quiet, potent, a grounded force—
Blue eyes bright with hope's steady course.

He saw your wounds, silent, no words to spare,
Traced your scars like pain he could bear.

Howl for the Vanished

No vows, no lies,
he hunted those instead
Who carved your hurt, left wounds that bled.

His fists met flesh,
a crack of bone and will,
Justice rose up, sharp, unyielding, still.
His anger burned, yet calm and fiercely true,
A strength that fought to right the wrong for you.

You flinched at first, raw, scared, and worn,
Could his love mend or leave you more torn?
Was it a trick,
a hope that would betray?
Another stranger with eyes that sway?

His fight was for the pain you long endured,
The wounds that left your soul obscured.
Through his resolve,
you saw a truth take hold:
You're more than scars,
not your pain retold.

Howl for the Vanished

Too long you walked in a fog of deep hurt,
Soul worn thin, drenched in sorrow's dirt.
His love—a light
that pierced the bitter night—
Was safe, warm, and held you tight.

Now he stands calm, no fight in sight,
No anger, just hands to guide you right.
You fall, let go,
too weary to stand,
He catches you,
a soft and steady hand.
His heart, your heart, no longer roam—
Sweet girl, at last,
you've found your home.

Howl for the Vanished
Between You and the Dark

My loyalty's gravel—
shards of the men I used to be.
I buried them alone, silent,
kept walking.

In a bar full of noise,
or on worn wicker chairs
sipping coffee,
birds sing from old oak limbs—
still, I barely speak.

These piercing blues
are always hunting for you.
And when they land,
they circle you like wolves in moonlight,
bound by a hunger
only you can feed.

I drag your name
through every nightmare
without a sound.
You're the light
I thank God I found.

Howl for the Vanished

So when the world swings on you,
when sorrow drops like lead—
don't flinch.
Let it come.
I'll be there.

Won't say a word.
Won't move an inch.
Unless it's to keep life
from leaving marks on you
like the ones it carved into me.

I'll catch every tear
in the torn lining of this coat,
count them silent—
like debts I'm honored to carry.

Not to fix you.
But to make damn sure
you stand when the smoke clears,
that nothing this world drags you through
could ever blot out
the feral fire in your bones.

If your breath ever falters,
I won't beg you to fight—
I'll plant my feet between you and the dark
and dare it to take a step closer.

Howl for the Vanished
The Red Wolf's Vow

In midnight's jaws,
where shadows gnash,
A regal soul defies the lash,
Its oath outburns the starless skies—
Red wolf, endure, though lands dissolve.

Its howl, a spear through mankind's drone,
Rebukes the wilds we've left to moan;
No den defies the tides' cruel sweep,
Where shattered swamps in silence weep.
A red wolf, throned in pocosin's gloom,
Once ruled where deer met dusk's red doom;
Through rifled glades,
it stalks alone—
Red wolf, endure, though lands dissolve.

In city glare, it stands unbent,
A sovereign shade, by towers rent;
Its iron gaze, both fierce and grand,
Scorns coyote's snarl and bloodied land.
In dreams, it hunts the stars' lost flame,
Their glint a wound no night can tame;
Each hope, like cinders, chokes and falls—
Red wolf, endure, though lands dissolve.

Howl for the Vanished

For balance lost, it braves the fray,
Through poacher's shot and drowned decay;
No pack, no kin, to share its crown,
Its stoic heart burns proud, alone.
And as the heavens douse their glow,
Where guilt and ruin's tides overflow,
This red wolf, scarred, majestic, free,
Spits its vow at our decree—

Red wolf, endure, though lands dissolve.

Howl for the Vanished
I Don't Sleep

They gave up when the cost ran high.
Left you bleeding, let it die.
They buried truth in shallow ground,
too scared to hear that haunted sound.

They didn't help, they turned away—
let silence rot what couldn't stay.
They didn't clean the blood or pain.
They didn't speak. They broke the chain.

But you—
you bore what they erased.
You held the fire. You faced the waste.
You rose, not pure, but scorched and raw—
a living wound, a walking law.

You tried to say I wasn't real,
to fake your way through what you feel.
But I remember-
I don't sleep.
I'm the story that cuts too deep.

You prayed the past would stay in stone—
but I dug up what you disowned.
I'm not a ghost. I'm not a lie.
I'm the reason every mirror lies.

Howl for the Vanished
Aftermath

I'm not flesh.
I'm what stayed behind
when the body forgot how to lie.
I'm the glitch in the ritual—
a mouth that kept humming
after the song was forbidden.

You said, move on.
I did.
Right into the nerve
of what you buried.

You said, heal.
I tried.
But the wound remembered.

I didn't tear out my eyes.
I gave them to the quiet—
and silence flinched.
What stared back
wasn't reflection.
It was something
that had waited too long
to be named.

Howl for the Vanished

I don't write with ink.
I write with sleep-loss,
with salt,
with the muscle memory of flinching.

My voice doesn't echo.
It lingers
in rooms where truth rotted
and no one opened a window.

Want verses?
Here—
a throat that forgot how to open,
a breath that collapsed
before lungs could hold it.

There's no metaphor.
Just the sound
a name makes
when it's said too late.

This isn't for you.
It never was.
It's for the haints
who stayed quiet
so someone else could sleep.

Howl for the Vanished

The names don't ride on my back.
They live beneath my ribs.
They keep time.
They don't ask.

You whisper, Let them rest.
But they've never closed their eyes.

I didn't walk out of the abyss.
I stayed.
I let it name me.
And it spoke softly
when it did.

Howl for the Vanished
Devoured

They say a man can shift his fate,
can carve a path from ruin,
but this blackness chokes my throat,
no light can pierce rays through it.

Every vow I've shattered,
every scalding, wretched tear,
Stokes this burning rage,
that sears me year by year.

I claw at rusted chains,
No freedom in my screams,
Her laughter's jagged echo,
Slicing through my dreams.

This pain's a rabid demon,
Gorging on my soul,
A carcass stripped and bleeding,
No shred of self left to console.

Howl for the Vanished

Let the world keep turning,
I'm rotting out of time,
A wraith gnashing memories,
Gutted in my prime.

I spit at splintered glass,
Those dead, unseeing eyes,
Devoured by this anguish,
Beneath a sky of knives.

Howl for the Vanished
Bitter Streams

She wore a dress of pearl white,
we argued in the dying light.
I said some things I can't unsay,
She turned and ran that final day.

The river's edge, the moon so cold,
She slipped beneath the waters's hold.
I heard her scream,
I felt her go,
In the dark, relentless flow.

I dove in, my heart a stone,
The water's chill cut to the bone.
I reached but failed to pull her near,
The river claimed what I held dear.

Now every night I see her there,
A ghost with water in her hair.
She calls my name in mournful tones,
Her voice,
the wind When I'm alone.

Howl for the Vanished

I taste her kiss in bitter streams,
I see her face in fevered dreams.
The river's hymn, my constant sin,
Now all I own
is a soul condemned.

Howl for the Vanished
Masks of Sin

I'm past repair, beyond the patch,
A busted lock with no more latch.
The light went out, the wires frayed,
What's left of me was built to fade.

I used to dream in softer tones,
Now trauma rattles through my bones.
Where most feel hope, I feel the void,
A life only I could destroy.

The charm is gone, the grin is dead,
I speak like death, not words just dread.
No velvet voice, no lover's role,
Just gravel caught in a blackened soul.

I've worn fake smiles like masks of sin,
now see no point in fitting in.
I'd rather rot than play it sweet,
I talk through teeth
all bloodied.

Howl for the Vanished

You left, I learned what truth can mean,
We danced in chains not golden rings,
Now I don't trust Any pretty things.

The anger grows beneath my ribs,
A storm that claws and never gives.
I drink to dull, I smoke to breathe,
Still haunted by the ones who leave.

I'm calloused, cold and war worn,
A soul that mercy don't reach for.
And still I search some godforsaken sky
For something real before I die.

But hell won't take what won't stay down,
So I remain,
too rough to drown.

Howl for the Vanished
The Frogs Sing Anyway

When the sky throws a tantrum,
ripping through Eastern Tennessee,
its rage spent—
mud and broken branches left behind.

The frogs—
slimy little dreamers—
croak their wild, throaty hum,
a secret locked inside my skin.

I sit here, coffee scalding my throat,
fist clenched—
swallowing a scream.

Those frogs—soft things,
I won't let out the part of me that still listens,
still feels the world's pulse in the wet dark.

Howl for the Vanished

I tell myself I'm hard, calloused as old leather—
but those damn frogs sing,
stubborn and aching,
a hymn that doesn't beg,
doesn't break.

And somehow—
somehow, I don't hate it.
Maybe, just maybe,
there's something left in me—
a croak waiting to rise.

Howl for the Vanished
Unshaken

When the fire comes, and the sky burns red,
will you stand still or bow your head?

When the winds howl, when the lines all blur,
will you stand firm as the cowards stir?

Not born of stone, not made of steel,
but something harder, raw, and real.

Not seeking praise, nor fearing scorn—
Just walking through the blaze, war-worn.

Can you live unseen, let the world forget your name,
and never once demand acclaim?

Can you lose it all, with will unbroken,
and build again, from what's been broken?

Will you speak truth when liars reign,
hold your ground beneath the strain?

Howl for the Vanished

Will you bear loss and not retreat,
still planting roots beneath defeat?

Can you throw the dice, stake your heart,
watch it shatter, then restart?

And if they mock or fear your form,
will you go on—
proud, stoic, worn?

Can you walk through crowds and stay your own,
not swayed by need, nor throne?

Then what you are no man can break,
no lie can bend, no storm can shake.

Not built for mercy, not chained to fate—
you walk through fire, and own your weight.

Howl for the Vanished
Red Wolf's Kin

Its howl, a torch through mankind's din,
It mourns the pack by rifles thinned
A regal soul defies abyss—
Red wolf, survive, though rivers die.

A red wolf, crowned in Clinch's gloom,
Once reigned where nutria
fled through reeds that twist;
Through coyote's sneer,
it stalks alone—
Red wolf, survive, though rivers die.

In neon glare, it strides unbowed,
A monarch lost, by screens overshadowed;
Its iron gaze, both fierce and grand,
Defies the grip of bloodied land.

In dreams, it hears the pack's last cry,
Their calls entombed where wetlands lie;
Each kin, like cinders,
chokes and drifts—
Red wolf, survive, though rivers die.

For kinship lost, it braves the fray,
Through poacher's shot and drowned decay;
No mate, no blood to share its pyre,
Its rebel heart burns past the mire.

And as the heavens dim their glow,
Where gunshots sealed the final woe,
This red wolf, scarred,
majestic, free,
Spits its vow at our decree—

Red wolf, survive, though rivers die.

Howl for the Vanished
The Hum

I sit in this room.
The world hums outside—
kids chasing kites, lovers trading whispers,
dogs barking at nothing.

I was never wired for that noise.
Even as a boy, I stood apart,
watching clouds form into shapes
no one else saw.

I'd rather shove a glowing branding iron
down my throat
than suffer through pointless pleasantries.
Small talk is torture.

My head—a busted radio,
tuned to a station that doesn't exist.
They moved in packs.
Laughter—coins clinking in a jar.

Lives stitched together, seamless.
I didn't fit. Still don't.
I sat on curbs, counted cracks in concrete,
while they ran, shouted,
belonged.

Howl for the Vanished

The air around me felt heavier,
carrying a secret I couldn't shake,
a pulse whispering—
"You're not them. You never will be."

Now I walk the city at midnight—
past bars glowing like bad ideas,
past strangers spilling secrets to strangers
they'll never see again.

Neon hums, promising love,
promising meaning,
promising lies.
I don't buy it. Never did.

I'm the guy who orders another drink,
watches ice melt—
sees a universe in the glass.
Planets spinning, stars collapsing,
none of it touching me.

There's a weight in my soul—
not sorrow, not exactly.
More like a shadow stitched to my heels,
trailing me from childhood's crooked streets
to this rented room,
It's walls peeling like old wounds

Howl for the Vanished

I was born with it—
the hum, the ache,
the thing that won't name itself.

It's how I see the world—
not a stage, but a busted machine,
gears grinding, spitting sparks,
while I stand outside,
hands in my pockets,
watching it turn without me.

I write on napkins—
scraps stained with coffee,
chasing the thing that's always been off.

The moon's a drunk, leering down.
And I'm down here, leering back.

Alone. Just alone.

Howl for the Vanished
Held What Broke Better Men

They say the Lord moves slow but right,
but life don't pause for holy light.
I learned that young in a broke-down town,
where dreams don't float—
they just drown.

I don't cry; I choke the pain,
pass that house where haints still curse my name.
Her fevered hand slipped as the light burned out—
now love's just a lie fools sing about.

She called me home in her last breath.
I lit a smoke, stared down death.
His eyes were abyss—but he just passed me by,
left me to rot beneath her sky.

I don't wear grace—just regret,
like barbed wire around my neck.
The stars don't shine where I lay my head—
just busted signs and walking dead.

Howl for the Vanished

Don't preach to me of clean or damned—
I've bled for both with these scarred hands.
Not proud, not fake,
I'm the scream silence shapes
in empty rooms where floorboards ache.

I've walked through hell and didn't break—
outdrew death with no mistake.
Heaven won't have me.
Hell won't dare.
Even the devil won't meet my stare.

I've stitched my wounds with broken vows,
buried guilt in burned-out towns.
The wind don't whisper—it howls my name,
and every mile just feeds the flame.

Don't lay me down with peace or pride—
just leave my boots where wolves won't hide.
I ain't the best, but I don't bend—
I've held what broke far better men.

Howl for the Vanished
Loyalty Is Quiet

If you have more friends than fingers—
Start counting backwards.

Mow the grass, trim the fat,
but snakes don't die,
they shed—
they return—
they wait.

They sharpen their grins,
polish their knives,
pour the drinks,
watch you drown.

Snakes don't bite for hunger—
they bite for sport.
They sink their teeth,
then call it mercy.

They talk redemption,
but wear your blood like perfume.
They slit your throat,
then ask why you don't speak.
They watch you burn,
then sell the ashes.

Howl for the Vanished

And when the embers cool,
when the dust settles,
they'll tell stories—
"We stood by you."

As if ghosts hold swords,
as if echoes make shields.

Loyalty isn't loud.
It doesn't boast,
doesn't promise,
doesn't ask for credit.
It stands when the ground crumbles,
when the knife is inches deep,
when silence
is the only truth left standing.

Snakes don't die.
The wise don't kill them—
they walk differently.

Howl for the Vanished
Porchlight

I was born with frost behind my eyes,
A restless wind beneath my skin.
I never stayed—
I cut my ties,
Too sharp to let them ever win.

I chased the roads, ignored the signs,
Left love like notes I'd never read.
Each town a blur between the lines,
I lived to leave—
a rambler's tread.

Your porch light cut through all the noise,
A glow that held when nothing did.
You saw the truth behind my voice,
The hurt I buried, the weight I hid.

You swore I wouldn't see twenty-nine.
I laughed, I winked, then floored the gas.
The lines were thin—
I felt alive,
But highs like that don't ever last.

Howl for the Vanished

The forest floor, when autumn sheds gold
Can hush the hearts that never break,
Might warm the ones too cold to hold—
Yet I still ran from my mistakes.

Your porch light framed your face that night,
When I rolled back down your street.
It felt like home, the only site
Where a man like me might face defeat

Your arms were peace no road could give,
No whiskey, fight, or fleeting flame.
I'd trade it all to feel that bliss,
To be the boy who knew your gaze.

I lost myself in every dive,
In every lie I swore was true.
But you're the weight that keeps me tied,
The only light I'm tethered to.

Howl for the Vanished

Now here I am—
hands clenched, pulse unsteady,
A man carved in asphalt and regret.
Your porch light dims,
a stranger's shadow ready,
Your life has turned, the past reset.

He stepped forward—
a man I didn't know.
Your eyes held peace—
no trace of me.
I turned. I drove—

Now no whiskey, smoke, or road
can drown the ghost
I'll never flee.

Howl for the Vanished
You Saw a Lantern

I'll wear the black hat if you need a devil
to make your story easier to swallow.
I've been called worse
by folks who knew me less.

You knew me—
not the man you stitched from dreams,
but the one who walked in
scarred, smoking, tasting like whiskey—
all bite, no promises.

I never offered safety.
I never promised stillness.
All I gave you was a match and the truth—
that I was born wild, not built to be caged
or softened.

But you struck the spark anyway,
thinking love could outshine the storm in me—
like tenderness could tame a thing
made of ash and ruin.

Howl for the Vanished

Now you're choking
on the smoke of your own hoping,
carving my name into the Wreckage
like I was the one who lied.

It wasn't me you fell for, was it?
It was the rumor, the thrill—
the way my name cut your tongue.

It's easier, I guess—
to make me the storm
than admit you loved the fire
while praying for rain.

I never wore a mask.
You just kept staring at the flame
and swearing you saw a lantern.
I wasn't hiding.
I was just too untamed
for the story you wanted to tell.

Howl for the Vanished
Bittersweet Realization

There's a thing in me,
small, quiet—
soft like old whiskey,
a shadow I never knew
until it left.

It sat at my table once,
between the unpaid bills,
the empty glass,
the cigarette burned too low.

Never spoke.
Just lingered, just stayed.

And when it walked out,
when the mornings grew sharp,
when the laughter thinned,
I knew—
that was happiness.
That was the thing I had
that kept me warm.

Howl for the Vanished
Tides of Eternal Night

The trembling stars,
tides that crash on
endless shores.
Fierce as fear's abyss,
soft as morning's hush—

I wandered ages,
lost in dark dreams,
adrift in unborn realms
where consciousness
learns to breathe.

Seeking what burns bright,
yet cloaked in eternal night,
until time's returning gravity
pierced the cosmic tide.

My soul, now caught in its pull.
The stars, the tides, the night—
never distant,
never lost.
Always, they have been you.

Howl for the Vanished
Smiling for the Strings

You're an outlaw.
Well... at least you used to be.

Since when did blending in
become your dream?
You swore you'd never chase
some mundane idea of "clean."

What happened to that fire?
The one behind your eyes—
that said you'd rather die
than live a pretty 9 to 5 lie.

Can you even remember
who you were
before they carved your edges off
and called the hollow healing?
Before you traded freedom—
a man unbound by their rigid rules.

Howl for the Vanished

You had a rebel soul—
not built to please, beg, or bend.
But now you echo
the very voices
you used to offend.

You've worn the mask so long,
it's fused to your skin.
Now you call it "growth,"
but I see the sin.

You forgot who you are.
And worse—
you stopped trying to remember.
Lost your spark
and became what you swore
you'd never be—
a dancing puppet,
smiling for the strings.

But I noticed how
that practiced smile faded
when I called you
by who you used to be.

Howl for the Vanished
Standing on Ruins

I dream of wings, but none unfold—
just heavy bones, a weathered soul.
The world is stitched
with silent screams;
they say it heals—
but that's yet to be seen.

I speak, but words just rot away,
drift like smoke, then fade to gray.
If you had worn
this weight awhile,
you'd learn to shape
a bitter smile.

Time don't mend what's lived all wrong—
it drags the hurt, just strings it along.
I lit my past
and watched it burn—
fire don't care
or show concern.

Howl for the Vanished

The road grows thin where no one goes,
lined with rust and orphaned crows.
No signs, no maps,
just beaten ground—
I walk 'til nothing turns around.

From shouting loud to internal screams,
I didn't grow wise—
I just lost sleep.
The man I am don't beg to know;
he's carved from loss
and calloused souls.

So I'll stay here—
I've set my terms
with ash and dust and things that squirm.
If death should come, it comes alone—
we've danced before.
I'm 1-0.

The past still breathes beneath my boots—
a field of graves without their roots.
And though I stand, I do not roam;
I stand on ruins—
I call them home.

Howl for the Vanished
The Void

You wore your pain like battered steel,
A man who faced too much to kneel.
Your eyes held storms that wouldn't break,
A hardened soul that wouldn't shake.

Each hook life threw, you faced head on,
A silent war fought far too long.
The darkness tried to claim you whole,
But never broke your stubborn soul.

Yet fast-lived years left their mark,
And now you have a tired heart.
You faced the void without a sound,
And slipped away without a crowd.

Now grief's a blade that steals my breath,
A hollow ache that chokes my chest.
Our songs, they cut with every chord,
Each note a wound, each verse a sword.

Howl for the Vanished

I curse the night, I curse this pain
That claws beneath my skin again.
This rage I wear like weathered steel
  Is every fight you couldn't heal.

Your son, your niece now raise their own,
  Your nephew speaks in rebel tones.
A kindred fire burns fierce and true—
The flame he carries comes from you.

I knew the scars you wouldn't show,
  The heavy truths you never told.
  I carry you like loaded lead,
  And keep my big iron close—
      like you said.

Your name's a torch no grave can claim,
  You never bent, you'll never fade.
  Death's cold victory stands denied—
    Your legend lives.
    Your spirit rides.

Howl for the Vanished
Certainty's End

Another day stretches forward,
a silent road to the scaffold.
I walk.

the saints murmur,
palms folded, lips moving,
but their weight is not mine.

this life was forged—
iron, silence, breath.
every step deliberate.
every choice made.

I did not stumble here.
I do not ask to be spared.
no plea, no mercy—
only the certainty,
of what was always mine to walk.

Howl for the Vanished
Heavens Haze

1 a.m., the static's loud—
TV preaching to a crowd.
There's no rest, just fight or flight;
truth hits harder late at night.

The mirror's cracked, my eyes are red,
ghosts are dancing in my head.
You said I didn't know to care—
I lit a smoke and left it there.

Your boots still sit by the front door,
but you don't walk this hardwood no more.
Death don't knock—
it kicks straight through,
and leaves the living black and blue.

I prayed with crimson fists
not for peace, just strength to win.
The Bible's torn but caught my screams,
half in rage, half in grief.

Howl for the Vanished

No prayers, no last words.
but for a moment—
just one—
I lift my gaze to the crowd,
searching for a familiar face.

there is none.
so I step forward.
and that is the end of it.

Howl for the Vanished

The whiskey burns, but it can't touch
the kind of pain that cuts this much.
I'd sell the stars, I'd bleed for days,
to see your face
through Heaven's haze.

The world still spins, the sun still sets—
but I ain't breathed without regret.

If I could steal just one more day,
I'd raise you up—come what may.
But death don't deal, and time won't bend;
it just leaves you bitter
in the end.

Howl for the Vanished
Where the Honeysuckle Grows

My mind's gone si'gogglin',
haven't walked the line since I's nine—
been trouble ever since.

My memory's all cattywompus—
I don't dwell on no burnt bridge.

You vanished—
hell, only thing to ever catch me off guard...
I'd've sworn you were heaven's gift.

They say I sit talkin' to myself,
say I drink to forget.
But I remember every off-key breath,
every word said.

They whisper I'm hollow,
say I checked out long ago.
But I still see your shadow,
where the honeysuckle grows.

Howl for the Vanished

(So let 'em talk.)

I expect no more
from cowards I once called friends.

I ain't some ghost of what I lost—
I forge this life with my own blood.
Not yours.
Not theirs.
Mine.

I chose roads no sane man dared,
under cold, pale moons and howling storms,
fought battles, held the damn line
when all the honorable,
"good men" fell short.

And I'm proud of every mark,
every scar they look down on.

No fate,
no destiny,
writes my last line.

I decide where I stand.
Still reckon I've got ground to cover.
I ain't done leavin' tracks just yet.

Howl for the Vanished
Red Wolf's Ghost

In shadow's grip, where specters moan,
My guilt stalks through the pocosin's throne;
Its eyes, like coals, ignite my dread—
Red wolf runs free,
though I struck you dead.

My rifle's crack still scars the air,
Its echo haunts the wild's despair;
No peace outruns the tide's grim swell,
Where marsh birds flee the wolf's last knell.

A red wolf, crowned in Clinch's mist,
Once roamed
where nutria scattered, swift and missed;
Through Albemarle's mire, I stilled its breath—
Red wolf runs free,
though I struck you dead.

In neon's glow, its shade won't flee,
A monarch's glare burns holes in me;
Its stoic wrath, both fierce and grand,
Condemns the blood upon my hand.

Howl for the Vanished

In dreams, I trace its vanished scent,
Their trails erased where rivers bent;
Each kin, like ash, dissolves in flight—
    Red wolf runs free,
    though I struck you dead.

For balance slain, I face the pyre,
Through coyote's scorn and drowned desire;
No mercy calms this searing woe,
Its ghostly howl makes rivers slow.

And as the heavens veil their flame,
Its blood still stains the tides that shame—
This red wolf, scarred, majestic, free,
Stalks my soul eternally—

    Red wolf runs free,
    though I struck you dead.

Howl for the Vanished
Old Souls

In all my years, you were a flicker
in the hush—
a flame I never reached for,
a fire I never wrote.

No one can brace for a fall
like ours—
reckless, raw—
your laughter a pulse
that cracked my frozen soul.

You didn't just enter—
you unmade my frame,
redrew the walls
with a name I whispered blind.

Our souls—
old, wary—
knew each other's shape,
spoke in a way
no barrier could change.

Howl for the Vanished

I lied like a coward,
swore it didn't cut—
as if time could soften
what knows it was once whole.

But we're done playing brave,
smothering the ache—
your absence a hole
in a heart that won't heal.

Still, I carry the remnants,
scarred deep, burning dim—
your touch still a whisper
beneath my ribs.

In all my years, you stay—
not just memory,
but the wound that won't close,
the love I can't unlive.

Howl for the Vanished
Middle of the End

Something slips through my fingers—
worse than having nothing at all.
I get mad at the sun shining,
blame my deadbeat dad for all the lying.

I feed myself stories
just to get through the rut.
Blame the rotgut bottle—
the dead weight in my blood.
I stitch up my wounds
with needles of liquid shame,
as the walls whisper my tormented name.

I fill my skull
with prescription haze,
forget how to cry,
but I remember the pain.
Still grind my teeth
when her voice fills the air,
still swallow fire
because I used to care.

Howl for the Vanished

Pain doesn't scream—
it slithers, it waits,
turns the days into months,
makes bright colors fade.
I sit through the morning
with weight in my chest.
Call it "healing,"
God knows I'm doing my best.

I'm not old,
but rot like a man long betrayed.
Still crave glory,
but can't accept praise.
But hey—
I can eat now,
I can sleep through the night...
Must count for something
in this godawful life.

I see the end—
and it looks just the same.
Nothing changes,
but the size of the cage.

Howl for the Vanished
I Stayed

My bloodline was carved from these mountains—
like the first cut of coal—
before they took her timber,
her marrow, her soul.

Before they paved over haints and hollers,
before they sank drills where no man should go.
Back when chestnuts still whispered warnings,
and rivers carried healing springs of old.

They took what they could carry—
the ginseng, the red wolves,
the lush green loblolly nestled between her ribs.
Left her naked—
degraded—
with her skin torn and traded,
nothing but wind
where her lullabies lived.

I stayed.

Howl for the Vanished

Not 'cause the land is mine—
these mountains are too ancient, too majestic
for any man to claim with deed or dollar.
But like many, I've known them—
loved them, called them home.

She holds me still—
not soft, but true.
A mother carved from stone
who never turned me loose.

There's a shaft sealed shut
where the ground still hums—
the company closed it
after the dead wouldn't rest.

Now the wind down there
don't sound like wind.
It sounds like remembering.

Howl for the Vanished

I stayed not from fear,
but because leaving
would be the final theft—
the last thing taken from a place
that has already given everything.

Some debts can only be paid in presence.
Some wounds can only heal
if witnessed.

And when I'm gone,
who will know the difference
between the wind
and the remembering?

Howl for the Vanished
Under These Oaks

Papaw,
you of all people knew
your only son's only son
was bound to be a little rebellious—
tokin' poison in the neighbor's yard,
hard-headed, sneaking smokes
behind the old shed,
where wild grass knotted secrets.

You'd sit there, wisdom-worn,
eyes cracked like old leather,
watching me stumble through the mess
I called freedom—
knowing some roads carve resilience,
some just scars.
You walked both. You never warned me,
just watched, just waited.

Howl for the Vanished

"Boy," your voice
rough as frost-split stone,
"no rebellion's new under these oaks."
And I'd laugh,
thinking I burned brighter
than all the fools before me,
while the streetlights dimmed
and the night unraveled
every reckless plan I had.

Papaw,
you saw the seasons in me—
rebellion, a young man's fire,
crackling in the soul, thawing to truth,
paid in bruises and choices that burn,
in roots that grip
when the dust finally settles.

Now I kneel here,
in the hush of the woods,
your blood a ghost
beneath my trembling hands—
hard-headed still,
tokin' these killers.

Howl for the Vanished

I don't know what I came here for.
Maybe just to hear myself say it—
how the nights feel longer,
how the streetlights don't flare the same,
how I keep turning
like you're still behind me,
waiting with that knowing look.

I could ask the wind if you're listening,
but I already know better.
So I sit, talking anyway,
like a boy who thought he knew
what fire was.

Howl for the Vanished
Still Breathing

Son, how the hell are you still breathing?
Men twice your size have cracked in half
under less than what you carry—
pain so deep it fused to your bones,
grew into the marrow,
made a home of your spine.

Boy, how did you survive
those nights you weren't even living—
just burning through anything
to feel something
for five fucking minutes?

Were you out on the road,
doing anything to outrun
the demons that moved in
and changed the locks
on your own damn mind?

Howl for the Vanished

I swear, I never saw you lose a fight
with anyone but your reflection.
So what's changed?
You used to speak like thunder,
now you whisper like a prayer—
like too many words
might wake the ghosts
you finally got to sleep.

I always hoped
your wounds would quiet with time,
that scars would turn to stories
you could tell without bleeding.

But some folks don't break all at once—
they crack slow,
a little more each day.
And sometimes,
the cruelest kind of living
is carrying the parts of yourself
that didn't survive,
even though you did.

Howl for the Vanished
What a Man Ought To

I came up hard where the cold winds bite,
where wrong feels right in the dead of night.

I fought for mine when the law turned blind—
not for glory, not for pride,
just to keep our way alive.

I've done what I had to.
I carry the weight.
I own the blame.
There's blood on my hands I can't erase,
but I'd do it again to keep them safe.

The past don't sleep—
it creeps, it calls,
like names carved deep in old stone walls.
I stood my ground when times got rough.
Sometimes, surviving has to be enough.

Howl for the Vanished

These hills remember every name.
They whisper truth.
They don't play games.
I walk with ghosts, but I don't hide.
My sins, my scars,
they walk beside.

I don't want peace if it costs my kin.
I'd gladly fall so they could live.

So when I'm gone, don't call me brave.
Just say I gave all I had to give.
Say I was hard, but I was true.
Say I did
what a man ought to.

Howl for the Vanished
Spark to Cinder

She was my last dawn, a gleam by the Hiwasse—
her light pierced the gloom where old shadows flinch.
My soul was caked in soot, bitter with sting.
I crushed her bright hymn,
broke the joy she could bring.

Her spark to cinder, I turned to bleak dust—
last grace in my dark, now a grave of my trust.

Her voice charmed the river,
stirred its mournful cold flow,
while I fed my own hate in a shack's ashen glow.
These hills hold their ghosts, they shoulder my sin.
I scarred her pure heart with the venom within.

Her spark to cinder, I burned to grim ash—
last star in my night, scarred by my wretched lash.

Howl for the Vanished

No flask drowns the guilt that gnaws deep in my core,
Just crows by the Hiwasse, singing grief's bitter score.
She's fled these cursed ridges,
found light that won't wane,
I'm chained to my ruin,
where no mercy remains.

Her spark to cinder, I forged in grim ire—
last good in my world, lost to my own fire.

Her love was my refuge, now bitter as frost.
I'm a wraith in the fog, bearing ruin's full cost.

Spark to cinder—
my throne's a jagged stone.
In these deathless old hills,
I'm damned and alone.

Howl for the Vanished
Bloodshot Dawns

Neon bleeds like a busted vein,
staining alley walls and windowpanes.
This lonesome stretch just won't relent—
beneath a sky too cold to repent.

Mama said, "You see too much,"
like truth was light—but it burns to touch.
This gift don't lift—it drags me low,
through towns where haints outnumber hope.

I walk the edge 'tween man and myth,
reaching for what don't exist.
Whiskey don't heal—
just salts the pain.
I drink to forget, then feel it again.

They preach success to the desperate and young,
but I've starved on dreams with a bitter tongue.
It climbs my ribs like a thorn-fed vine,
choking out the fire it was meant to refine.

Howl for the Vanished

I keep on movin'—
new towns, same sin,
same ceilings crack, but never give in.
My hands stay bruised, my voice runs thin,
from all I've lost and where I've been.

This world don't build no homes for me—
just bloodshot dawns and memories.

Howl for the Vanished
Morgan Dollars

If every day's a Morgan dollar
I trade for her a better life,
then I ain't just a rail spike driver—
I'm the finest one to touch a spike.

My father drove these same steel crosses
through ground his father broke before,
but I drive deeper, counting losses
in the coins I lay in store.

I wake before the sun remembers
to bleed its light through mountain stone,
drive steel through frostbit earth and embers,
and curse the vow I made alone.

My hands are maps of busted blisters,
my spine's a ledger tallied clean—
one coin per day, a silver whisper
toward a dream she's never seen.

Howl for the Vanished

The rails stretch east to cities golden,
    west to shores I'll never see—
each spike I set's a door that's closing,
    each mile I build ain't built for me.

She used to hum while washing dishes—
    some hymn her mother sang so sweet.
Now silence haunts my hollow wishes,
and rails grow long, through hollers steep.

But if the Lord is keepin' count,
    hammerin' nails in heaven's wood,
I hope He knows the true amount—
    I gave her more than flesh and blood.

I gave her roads I'll never travel,
    bridges spanning what I lack,
and when these bones turn dust and gravel,
    she'll ride the rails I hammered back.

Howl for the Vanished
Clean Sky

They sent me down at break of day,
With wage too low, and wolves to pay.
Walls groaned. Seams wept.
Firedamp curled itself and slept.

My lamp burned low, the shaft was tight,
The air ran thin, the floors weren't right.
The foreman said, "We'll shoot it blind."
He left the ghosts for us to find.

Three sixty-two at Monongah—
Forty-six when our shaft fell.
Numbers stamped on a cold report,
But every one had tales to tell:

Of coffee cooling by the door,
Of children's names, of Sunday light,
Of garden plots, of fishing holes,
Of dreams too big to have at night.

Howl for the Vanished

My daddy died with lungs gone black,
   Breath a whistle, thin and high.
I swore I'd break the family chain,
   But poverty don't hear you cry.

Twenty-five years underground—
   Odds say ten-to-one you'll die.
Your chest becomes a crypt unseen,
Your lungs the tombstones of your sky.

But evenings, when I rise,
   My daughter runs to meet my arms.
She don't see coal dust in my eyes,
Just Daddy, home and safe from harm.

Homework spread across the table,
   Her future bright as morning sun.
Each cough I swallow makes her able
   To be the first, not just someone

Howl for the Vanished

Who trades their body, breath, and years
To keep the lights on up above.
The mine takes lungs but cannot raze
The architecture of our love.

So when the black dust claims my chest,
And widow's tears replace my wage,
Know the weight I bore to rest
Bought her a turning of the page.

I ain't no hero cast in stone—
Just coal dust mixed with father's prayer,
That she might breathe what I've sown:
Clean sky, and choices, and fresh air.

Howl for the Vanished
Howl for the Vanished

I knew men once—
red wolves in human skin,
stalking through dusk's blood-wet pines,
their throats torn open
to a sickle moon.

They hunted—
not for nothing,
but for those with the same blood
singing in their veins—
sharp as flint—
bitter as sour mash,
their ribcages rattling
like storm-shook tin.

These men never knelt—
not unless the earth itself
cracked wide,
spilling its black heart.

Howl for the Vanished

Their voices—
thunder trapped in a mason jar.
Their eyes—
a glint of untamed country,
promising a fight
no city could cage.

But the wolves are ghosts now,
their howls snuffed in valleys and swamps,
chased to shadows
by asphalt and steel.

The men, too—
fading under neon's hum,
their boots no longer grinding red clay,
their songs—
that moon-cracked howl—
swallowed by glass towers
and prayers that flicker like bad bulbs.

Howl for the Vanished

They call it progress,
this taming of fang and fist.
I call it theft—
a slow extinction,
a world caged in concrete,
where ghosts forget
the taste of bone.

I pour a drink—
bourbon neat,
the color of Hiwassee river mud—
for my neighbor's shadow,
his growl drowned
in neon's drone.

I stand on this Tennessee ridge,
throat raw,
and howl for them all—
wolf and man,
their echoes thinning
like mist in the dark.

Howl for the Vanished

One last call—
futile as a spark in rain—
but I'll keep calling,
just to prove
the wild in me
still burns.

Howl for the Vanished
Afterword: The Fire Remembers

I wrote these words for no audience.
Not for applause. Not for comfort.
I wrote them because silence
rots a man from the inside.
Because grief has teeth.
Because love leaves scars.

If you found yourself here—
if some flicker of your own sorrow
caught fire in these lines—
know this:
You are not alone in the dark.
Not now. Not ever.

The world will tell you to forget.
To soften.
To bow.
Let it.

Somewhere deep within,
the wild in you remembers.
The fire in you waits.

Light it again.
Burn so bright the dark won't dare
swallow you whole.

— B.D. Lynn

Made in United States
Orlando, FL
17 August 2025